THANK YOU, LORD,
for My Home

THANK YOU, LORD,
for My Home

Gigi Graham Tchividjian

world wide
publications

1303 Hennepin Avenue,
Minneapolis, Minnesota 55403

ACKNOWLEDGMENTS

WHICH? by Dr. V. Raymond Edman. From *In Quietness and Confidence* by Victor Books. Used with permission. I DID NOT SAY . . . (originally titled: SILVER ANNIVERSARY) by Jane Merchant. From *Halfway up the Sky* by Jane Merchant. Published by Abingdon Press. Used through courtesy of Elizabeth Merchant. MY TALE WILL LEAVE NO ONE AGHAST . . . by Jane Merchant. Used through courtesy of Elizabeth Merchant. O LORD, BESTOW YOUR BLESSING by James J. Metcalfe. Copyrighted. Courtesy Field Enterprises, Inc. Our sincere thanks to the following authors whose addresses we were unable to locate: William F. Beck for LORD, THE RIVERS MAKE A NOISE . . . ; Amy Carmichael for I ASK THEE FOR A SELFLESS LOVE . . . ; LORD, IS ALL WELL? and NOT IN VAIN; Edwin Hodder for THY WORD IS LIKE A GARDEN, LORD; Martha Snell Nicholson for HIS PLAN FOR ME.

ISBN 0-89066-023-9

This special edition is reprinted by permission of
Ideals Publishing Corporation

Photograph opposite: The Graham home in Montreat, N.C.

To all of those who have faithfully done their part in providing and adding to the heritage that I have received; but especially to my Daddy, who taught me to look at things "with Eternity's values in view," to Mother, who for thirty-three years has given me the consistent example of living a life in total reliance upon the person of Jesus Christ, and to both of them because they introduced me to the One who has given me Eternal Life.

And to my husband Stephan, who asked me to share his heritage in this life and for Eternity, and provides the love, the leadership, and the godliness that makes it a joy to continue passing our God-given heritage on to our children.

Photograph opposite: The author with her husband, parents, and children following her oldest son's confirmation.

Contents

Photograph opposite: The front gate at the author's childhood home in Montreat, N.C.

Foreword

Stop your busy life for five minutes and ask yourself the question, "What is it that makes it all worthwhile and meaningful—the daily routines, the responsibilities, the little tasks that need to be done over and over again, the pains of the moments of loneliness and doubt?" I believe most of us, maybe all of us, realize that what does make it all worthwhile are our relationships, the relationships we have with our spouses, children, father and mother, our friends, and the very unique relationship all of us have been invited to have with our Heavenly Father and His children. I personally become every day more deeply convinced that the very fabric of my life is woven with the threads of the relationships I have formed over the years.

Each one is different; each one contributes a very special quality of color, texture, strength and design to the whole. There are, of course, some threads without which the fabric would unravel and become useless and meaningless. Without some others it would only lose some of its radiance and uniqueness.

Thank You, Lord, for My Home

Thank You, Lord, for My Home accepts the fact that God is the master weaver of our life and has chosen to use our family relationships to weave the beautiful cloth which would bring honor to Him. The times we learn to receive and learn to give, the parts of our inner selves that blossom in the rays of family love, and the pains inflicted by family neglect, all can be blended to form a person of compassion and character, when the Holy Spirit is allowed to heal, nurture and guide. Gigi has allowed our Lord to pursue this work in her life. I have witnessed her tears of discouragement and her smiles of gratitude. We have shared those moments when nothing seems right and those times when a look on one of the kids' faces makes it all worthwhile.

This book has been written with words drawn from Gigi's inner heart. She shares the love she has received in her home, the godly and yet very human example given by her father and mother and by her grandparents. But she goes beyond the comforts of looking back; she shares her present and her hopes for the future. She is honest and transparent; she asks the difficult questions a mother and wife would ask. She answers them when she has an answer, and she shares her faith that our Father will answer those for which she has not yet found her answer.

Read the book, look at the pictures, and while you do, please remember that God is writing a marvelous book about your own life, filled with pictures of those wonderful moments He has given you and your family.

One day it will be our privilege to share in the reading of that book with you.

Stephan Tchividjian

Gigi

by Ruth Bell Graham

Everybody should have one Gigi to raise. She was a terror, believe it or not. In fact, I remember coming home, I don't know where I'd been, and our maid met us at the door and said, "Mrs. Graham, I don't know what's getting into the children, but they went up to the neighbor's house and sassed her."

Well, now, this comes under moral issues, so I went upstairs with the little shoe tree and Gigi saw me coming. She was always the spokesman for the group; she was the one that usually thought up the mischief and got the others to carry it out. Basically she is a shy individual, but boy, can she think up the things. She heard me coming, so she started in before I even hit the door.

She said, "Mother, you can't blame us. It wasn't our fault. It was the devil! He, he's the one that got into us and he's the one that made us do it! Mother, you just can't blame us!"

And I said, "I realize, Gigi, that it was the devil. And what I'm aiming to do is to beat him out!" which I proceeded to do. I had to leave again for about two hours and when I came back, our maid said, "Mrs. Graham, I don't know what happened, but they've done the same thing over again."

Well, this time I shot up those steps, two at a time and Gigi heard me coming, and she started in.

"Mama, you can't blame me! You know it was the devil that got into us!"

All of a sudden she saw my face and said, "But Mother, as soon as he saw you coming, he left!"

So you see what I mean, everybody ought to have at least one Gigi.

I do not say
That there were no
misunderstandings,
discontents,
and hurts.
I would it had been so.
Strange, how the heart
sometimes assents to angers
that the will asserts;
but these we learned
to live above.
I do not say
there were no hurts.
I say
they mattered less
than love.

> Jane Merchant

Preface

These few pages are only an attempt to show a glimpse of God's blessings in my life. I find too few words that adequately express my humble gratefulness to Him for choosing me and placing me where He did. It would be impossible to try and elaborate on all the warm open affection, the generosity, the truly humble spirit, and the singleness of purpose that I saw exemplified in Daddy. Or the love, understanding, patience, hours of time, and example of a truly godly woman that I saw in Mother. Or, on all the other blessings and spiritual riches that I have received and continue to receive from my home. It would be difficult, because I do not find it easy to express in either word or deed all that is deepest in my heart. So I trust that as you turn these pages, you will both read the lines and between them and glimpse a small portion of the grace of God in my life.

Why Have a Home?

I never like to share too much about myself because I have never wanted anyone to know more about Gigi Graham Tchividjian than about the Lord Jesus Christ. But I thought I would just share a few of my thoughts about why I am so grateful that I had a home, and why I myself chose to have a home. And as you read, I pray that the Holy Spirit will cause Gigi to decrease and the Lord Jesus to increase.

First, let me state emphatically that I have in no way arrived. Once on a sign, I read that a saint was a sinner revised and edited, and I am still being revised and edited. I am a Christian, a wife, a daughter, a mother, and a friend, in progress. I still don't have it all together all the time, nor did my family while I was growing up. I was not born with a halo, as this book indicates.

A dear friend of mine, who is a wonderful Christian wife and mother, once said that she used to go around the house closing all the windows before she screamed at her children. Well, the only difference between my friend and myself is that I don't bother closing the windows. I am a normal daughter, a normal wife, and a normal mother. I fail often to live up to what I believe the Lord Jesus asks of me, and I often wonder if He will be able one day to say to me, "Well done, thou good and faithful servant." But, by His grace, and in His strength I am still in progress.

Finding Someone to Keep

One day I asked my children what they thought marriage was. My eldest, who was quite young then, said, "It's when you find somebody you want to keep." No wonder God told us to be as little children! But today in America, one out of two marriages ends in divorce. In looking through almost any newspaper, there are less requests for marriage licenses than requests for divorce. On a recent "Today Show," experts were discussing divorce and they said that the main cause for divorce today was selfishness; couples would rather switch than fight. Marriage, however, was not out according to these experts, because eighty percent of these same people remarried. A survey taken among college students showed that eighty-seven percent put a happy home as their number one goal in life.

Yet husbands are walking out more and more,

wives are leaving home and children. One woman who had decided to leave husband and children was quoted as saying, "I don't think marriage is a rewarding, fulfilling life. It is merely adequate and they are kidding themselves if they don't realize their need for more than just marriage in life." More and more women are seeking abortions. I was shocked the other day to read in our local paper's classified ad section at least eight large-print ads for "inexpensive termination of pregnancy." And even children are running away from home at earlier and earlier ages.

So, why have a home? What is a home? What is a family?

What Is a Family?

Webster's *Dictionary* says that a family is "a group of persons of common ancestry or a group of individuals living under one roof and under one head." No wonder the family is under question. I, too, would ask the question, "Why have a home?" if that were all there was. Webster's goes on to define "home" as "the house where one lives, the country or place where one lives, or where one's ancestors lived. The social unit formed by a family living together in one dwelling." Is that it? I have been surprised to find out that for many, a home and family are not much more than the definition in *Webster's Dictionary*.

I hear many confess that they rarely, if ever, even eat as a family. Each one is off doing his or her own thing. Today, people are too busy and much too preoccupied with self to even eat a meal together, much less spend an evening in conversation. Do you really know what makes the other members of your family happy? Or if one is really hurting? Or what their goals and values are?

Edith Schaeffer, in her book *What Is a Family?*, compares a family to a mobile—moving, changing, constantly in motion, yet within the framework of a form. She says a family is "unity and diversity, form and freedom, togetherness and individuality, and a Christian family is a mobile blown by the gentle breeze of the Holy Spirit."

The Family Changes

Today we are moving, changing, constantly in motion, but we are losing the framework and the form. Traditions no longer have the same influence on families. Values are changing and there is a real lack of absolutes. Roles and responsibilities are changing. There is a lack of authority and respect.

Modern conveniences have alleviated much of the traditional work in a home, but modern society has placed many other outside pressures and responsibilities on the family. The pressure for Father to succeed and "get ahead," the pressure for Mother to have an occupation outside the home or to get involved in the community or the church. The pressure for the kids to do well in school, which today means being able to choose the right friends and to be able to say "no" to so many temptations, as well as excel in sports, not to mention the original

Photograph opposite: Overlooking the mountains of Montreat, N.C.

reason for their being in school in the first place. All of this is on top of all the normal everyday tensions and frictions of a normal homelife. How does one cope with all of this and still try to hang on to a "family," or is it worth the effort?

So many of these things are totally foreign to the home atmosphere in which I grew up just fifteen years ago; and yet, as a mother of six children (two of them teenagers) living in a large American city, I now face many of these growing problems of a transient society. The more problems I see and face, the more grateful I become for the homelife that I was privileged to have back in the mountains of North Carolina.

Which?

Which shall I choose today?

The hard or easy way;
To seek some soul to bless,
Or stay in idleness;
For some cause to sacrifice
Or simply close my eyes;
Work out God's plan for me,
Or set my passions free;
Climb upward on my knees,
Or only seek for ease;
Walk where the martyrs trod,
Or scorn the claims of God?

Lord, in my heart today,

I give Thee right of way,
Work both to will and do
And help me to be true.

Dr. V. Raymond Edman

Memories

My home provided a storehouse of happy memories. When I look back, I realize that my home provided for my physical, emotional, material, and most of all, my spiritual needs. My home had form, and the framework was my godly Christian heritage.

The first thing that comes to my mind when I think how grateful I am that I had a home is my Christian heritage. In Jeremiah we read, "Before I formed you in the womb I knew you, before you were born, I set you apart." I believe that God knew me before I was even formed, and that He had a plan for my life. I do not believe for a moment that I was conceived or born by accident; nor do I believe that I was placed by accident into my family.

I was born into a family that prayed for me and loved me before I ever entered this world, especially since my parents had been told that they would probably never be able to have children. All of my

Photograph opposite: The author as a young girl helping her brother.

aunts and uncles, my grandparents, and my parents loved and served the Lord. They provided me with a vital, living example of what true Christianity is all about. It is a Life, a life of joyous commitment, not just a religion. I am still awed by this, because the Bible says in Luke, "that to whom much is given much will be required." In the Old Testament, we often see and read of the godly heritage of Israel; and yet, we also read how often they failed and disappointed the Lord. I know that I fail Him often. I doubt or question at times, I struggle at other times; but I will be forever grateful for my godly heritage.

The Devil Didn't Have a Chance

Why have a home? As I said, my godly heritage began before I was born, but it became a personal reality to me when, at the age of four, I gave my heart and my life to Jesus Christ. I was quite ill, and my mother was worried and afraid that I might die. So she decided to tell me more about Jesus and how I could make Him a part of my life forever. She came to my room, sat beside me on the bed, and began to tell me how much God loved me. She explained to me that God loved me so very much that He sent His only Son Jesus Christ to die on the cross for me and to take away all of my badness. The only thing I had to do was to tell Him that I was sorry and ask Him to forgive my badness; and that if I would do that He would come and live in my heart, and one day He

Photograph opposite: The author as a young girl with her brother.

would take me to heaven to live with Him forever. So I did just that. In very simple, childlike faith that day, I asked Jesus into my heart and into my life.

Now, in looking back, I realize that I could have said no to Jesus that day; or later, as I became an adult, I could have dismissed that day as just a childish experience forced upon me by my mother. But the Bible says in Philippians 1:6, "He that hath begun a good work in you, will perform it until the day of Jesus Christ." In other words, the Holy Spirit started something that day and He will continue to revise and edit and prune and refine me until Jesus Himself returns, and "I shall be like Him for I shall see Him as He is." So by the grace of God and the steadfast, faithful prayers and teaching of my godly family, my godly heritage, I somehow think that the devil just didn't have a chance with me.

The Extended Family

When it became apparent early in my life that Daddy was going to be away from home much of the time, he decided to let Mother choose where she would like to live. She chose a little cove in the mountains of North Carolina called Montreat. It was a small community, largely comprised of retired Presbyterian missionaries in the winter months and a conference center in the summer months. She chose this little place because my grandfather, a retired medical missionary and a surgeon, still had

Photograph opposite: Dr. Graham walking with his children.

a practice in Asheville not too far away; and they had chosen Montreat as their home. With Daddy away so often, Mother felt that it would be wise to settle near her parents; so we bought and lived in the little house right across the street from them.

The years have proven over and over again that the Holy Spirit was guiding Mother in that important decision. I grew up knowing all the privileges and blessings of the extended family. I could run over to my grandparents, across the little stream and across the street, down to their back door which was never closed, any time I wished. My grandparents made it a part of their ministry to help Mother raise us children. I will never be grateful enough for the influence that my grandparents had on my life, and the forming of my values and character. My Christian heritage was further enlarged by all the contacts that I had with all the dear saints of God who lived in our small community. And also, by the fact that my paternal grandparents lived on a dairy farm just two hours away.

Today, in our transient society, we are moving away from the meaningful concept of the extended family. We don't know our aunts and uncles, nor our cousins. We as a family decided to try to meet once a year for a "family reunion" to help close the gaps that develop when families are spread apart as we now are. This last year, my husband Stephan and I felt this to be so important that we chose to move

closer to family. As much as we value the independence of our own family unit, we also value greatly the larger family, the valuable advice of parents, the care and concern of brothers and sisters, the influence of all the family members on the children. What a source of strength and support this provides, especially in times of decision or crisis. And what a source of friendship and fellowship, diversity and unity, togetherness and individuality. That is what it is all about. Now there are also some heated discussions and everything is not always peaceful agreement. But this is good as long as you can learn to disagree pleasantly.

Perhaps we have an unusual family, but it didn't just happen all by itself. It has taken quite a few years of hard work, a lot of giving and taking, a lot of learning to appreciate the individual God-given differences, and a lot of acceptance. Stephan's family is from Armenia and Switzerland, and when I joined his family you can well imagine the adjustments for all involved. Yet because we valued the individual and the family, we all worked, and did a lot of learning, and it has been worth every effort.

One night at dinner we were discussing families and family life, and my oldest son said that he thought that the family included all the elements of society miniaturized. I learned and received much from my family as I was growing up; and that hasn't diminished, it has only changed a bit in form as we

have all changed and matured. And how I thank God for my family!

Now I am very aware that this type of Christian heritage is more the exception than the rule. There are very few of us that could claim such a heritage. Yet there is not a single one of us that is not privileged to start such a heritage for our own children and our own grandchildren by making sure of our own relationship with Jesus Christ.

Home Provides Security

Another reason I am so grateful I had a home is the security it provided for me. One day around the table, I asked my children what a home was to them. My little four-year-old answered, "Mama, a home is a place where you come in out of the rain." And you know, I thought, that's it. Home is security, it is warmth, it is protection and reassurance; and in the Old Testament, God is often spoken of as the *El-Shaddai*, the Mother God—the all-sufficient one, protecting and providing. Outside the home the storms are fierce. We are often very ignorant of all the situations our family members have to face when they are away from the home: school and social pressure, job pressure, peer pressure, just to name a few. So how much more important it is for the home to provide security. Proverbs 31:18 in the Amplified version says, "Her lamp goes not out, but full of the oil of the Holy Spirit it burns on continu-

Photograph opposite: A rainy day at Montreat, N.C.

ally through the night of trouble, privation, or sorrow, warning away such robbers as fear, doubt, and distrust." What a beautiful responsibility and privilege we have as mothers and wives to provide an atmosphere such as this for our loved ones.

The privileges and tremendous responsibility of providing such influences and such an atmosphere are not just confined to the walls of our immediate homes. The repercussions are widespread and continue long after the initial influence, like the ripples that continue long after a stone is thrown into a quiet lake. These ripples are aided by a gentle breeze, and the same is true of the initial seed of godliness planted in a family and allowed to continue aided by the gentle breeze of the Holy Spirit. In my home it started many years ago, because my ancestors decided to put Jesus first in their lives.

A Christian Heritage

The ripples are continuing and growing ever larger and ever broader because of my family's faithfulness in passing down my godly heritage. And it will continue to grow, by the grace of God, as long as we who have received such a heritage are faithful in our personal relationship to Jesus Christ and to our God-given responsibilities in our homes. Stop for a moment and think of how many people will be influenced by just one child raised to love the Lord Jesus, a child who has been grounded in the living Word and has been given the living example of a godly mother. The potential influence of a faithful, god-fearing parent is unending, and the very staggering thought should make us reverence our job, and be grateful to God that He has entrusted us with so much responsibility.

We grandchildren once asked my paternal grand-mother (Mother Graham) how my grandfather and all of his family had come to know the Lord. She didn't want to say at first, but we pushed a bit, and we learned that my grandfather (Daddy Graham) and all of his family found the Lord through the quiet, sweet Christian example that Mother Graham lived before them in the home. Because of her quiet, faithful, godly living and example in that home, she was able to pass on the godly Christian heritage that I have received. What a privilege and respon-sibility was hers, and how grateful I am that she was faithful as a wife, a mother, and mother in-law.

Families Provide Love and Respect

Yes, home provided security. First, I was always secure in love and I knew that whatever I did I would always, always be loved. Oh, it was often tough love and never cheap sympathy; but my parents made it very clear that they always loved me, even if they didn't love what I did.

I always felt loved and accepted, even though I was often punished and corrected. My parents taught us from the very first that their type of love was the same love God has for us. God loves a sinner, but He hates sin. My uncle once said, "God loves us enough to accept us just the way we are, but He loves us too much to leave us there." My parents felt the same way.

Daddy, although away from home much of the time during my formative years, commanded a deep respect. We knew that he loved us more than anything in the world, and he demonstrated this love in many open, outward expressions. His very presence caused me to feel shame if I was naughty. Next to my desire to please the Lord, I wanted to please him. I remember one day, when I was still quite young, he arrived home from a trip a bit earlier than expected. I was in the process of doing something that I knew I shouldn't do. I can still remember how ashamed and sorry I was, and how guilty I felt as I ran down the drive and threw myself into his waiting arms.

The book of Proverbs is filled with the godly and practical wisdom of Solomon. As much of this godly, practical wisdom as was humanly possible was practiced in my home while I was growing up. My parents and my grandparents felt that godly, formative influences were necessary to cope with sinful enticements and that verses such as Proverbs 13:24, "He that spareth the rod hateth his son; but He that loveth him chasteneth him early," and Proverbs 22:15, "Foolishness is bound in the heart

Photograph opposite: Gigi and her father after he had baptized her.

of a child but the rod of correction shall drive it far from him," were to be taken quite literally. So, of course, we were spanked and punished. But as soon as we were punished, we were held, we were loved, we were kissed, we were forgiven, and we were never reminded of that fault again. It's the same with God. When God forgives, God chooses to forget. As Corrie ten Boom says, "He takes our sins and He buries them in the deepest sea and He puts up a sign, 'No Fishing Allowed!' "

As I Go on My Way

My life shall touch a dozen lives before this
   day is done,
Leave countless marks for good or ill ere
   sets this evening's sun.
Shall fair or foul its imprints prove, on those
   my life shall hail?
Shall benison my impress be, or shall blight
   prevail?

From out each point of contact of my life with
   other lives,
Glows ever that which helps the one who for
   the summit strives?
The troubled souls encountered, does it
   sweeten with its touch,
Or does it more embitter those embittered
   overmuch?

Does love through every handclasp flow
   in sympathy's caress?
Do those that I have greeted know a newborn
   hopefulness?
Are tolerance and charity the keynote of
   my song,
As I go plodding onward with earth's eager,
   anxious throng?

                          Strickland Gillilan

A Living Heritage

I was secure because my parents built up my confidence. They applied David's principle in raising his son Solomon, as stated in Psalm 72:15, "Prayer shall be made for him continually and daily shall he be praised." We were backed by prayer and encouraged by praise. This is so important, because if a child doesn't have these basic needs met at home, it won't be long before he or she is seeking them elsewhere. But even more than this, my parents taught us to seek and find our total confidence in the Lord. Proverbs 32:6 says, "The Lord shall be thy confidence," and Proverbs 14:26 says, "In the fear of the Lord is strong confidence, and His children shall have a place of refuge."

Examples of Disciplined Christians

Then we had examples. Mother has often said that the best way to make a child eat his dinner is to see his parents thoroughly enjoying theirs. And I firmly believe the main reason we all grew to love the Lord Jesus and to fear and reverence, God is that we saw all around us the examples of Christians thoroughly enjoying their faith. We had examples of happy, fun-loving, disciplined Christians. We had daily Bible readings; and when I say daily Bible reading or devotions, I do not mean a long drawn-out boring thing. It was a fun time. It was usually a hectic time because it was before we left for school in the morning; but it was fun and it was kept short. If Daddy were home, he would read a short passage of the Scripture or a Bible story and then lead a short prayer. We knelt for prayer; and sometimes if it got a little too long, my little brother would say, "Amen." In other words, "Daddy, that's long enough!" If Daddy weren't home, then Mother led the devotions.

We have continued this practice with our children. Usually we read the Bible and share with one another after supper in the evening, before we all scatter. It continues to be hectic but fun. It is often difficult because of the age differences to keep each one's attention; but we plug on, and it is very meaningful and rewarding to share spiritually together as a family. Usually Stephan reads from either the Bible or a Bible storybook. He reads a short passage, then usually asks a few questions. Or perhaps we will recite a Bible verse or each try to think of a verse or passage of Scripture that deals

Photograph opposite: Dr. Graham reading to his children.

with a certain subject, such as love or joy, etc. We have taught our children to each have a personal time alone with the Lord every day; sometimes we might ask each child to share with the family something that he or she has received in his or her personal time with the Lord. Or one member of the family might have a question about something he read in the Bible or a current issue that has spiritual implications. So we take time to discuss this. Devotions can certainly be a varied and fun, family time.

I believe the Bible teaches that the husband is the high priest of the family; but when Stephan is away, I usually lead the family in devotions. Also, as I tuck the children in bed at night, we talk together, recite verses and pray. So for those women whose husbands for some reason can't or won't take this responsibility, or for women raising a family alone, there are many ways to influence your children spiritually and set an example for them. Again, it was the example of seeing my family enjoy their personal time with the Lord that made me want to follow suit. I often stayed with my grandparents at night because they lived just across the street. I still remember coming down for breakfast and seeing my grandfather on his knees in prayer. Or going in to say "goodnight" to my mother and finding her on her knees in prayer, closing her day with the Lord. I have a sign on my desk that says, "If your day is hemmed in by prayer, it is less likely to unravel." I found this out by example and practice in my family.

As I was growing up, Sunday nights were very, very special family nights. My grandparents lived very close to us and helped raise us; they would come up every Sunday night, have supper with us; then we would gather around the grand piano and sing hymns and then play Bible games. I learned a great deal about the Bible from those Bible games.

Then we had humor, lots and lots of humor. Tension was often broken by a joke and we always, always tried to see the humorous side of even very difficult situations. Also, we were taught by example that a "soft answer turneth away wrath, but grievous words stir up anger" (Prov. 15:1). Christianity was anything but a boring religion to me. It was an exciting way of life. When we had either personal or family problems, we were taught to talk them over with our Heavenly Father. In fact, we were taught early to talk to God about everything and anything, from a major decision in our life, such as college or our future mates, to simply finding a parking space uptown. My parents and grandparents followed the Lord's teaching in Deuteronomy 6, "You must teach these laws to your children, talk about them when you are at home, or out for a walk, at bedtime, and first thing in the morning."

In other words, it became a part of our everyday life, and even now I don't separate my spiritual life from my daily life. I talk to the Lord while I'm driving my car to the shopping center or the grocery store, while I'm washing dishes or vacuuming; and I talk to the children about the Lord when I'm bathing them at night or when we're working in the garden together. I lived in Milwaukee, Wisconsin, for five years and it was a battle with the Lord and me every winter, but when spring came, I got so excited. On the first spring-like day, one year, I was out in my yard and I was really happy. I was raking, and my little four-year-old was with me, and every time I'd rake up the brown leaves, the little green grass was coming up. Every time I saw a new bud on the willow tree, I'd exclaim, "Oh, isn't it beautiful, isn't the grass lovely. Oh, look at the flowers!" Finally, my son looked at me and said, "Mama, thank God, not me." And he was right. You don't need lots of time to worship the Lord, just here a little and there a little.

Examples of Happy, Loving Marriages

Then we had examples of happy, loving marriages; of helpmeets not doormats. I often heard these wives disagree with their husbands, but pleasantly, and never with rollers in their hair. Mother taught us that if two people agree on everything, one of them is unnecessary; there should always be room for disagreement. Kahlil Gibran said, "Let there be spaces in your togetherness." But to dis-

51

agree pleasantly takes time, and the *right* time, not when both are tired and it is late. God has given women many charming ways to disagree. A smart woman will always try to look her best before bringing up a touchy subject, even a comb and a little lipstick can do miracles. Stephan often arrives just as I am fixing dinner. I usually try to freshen up before he arrives, but sometimes I haven't had a moment to myself. He sees me over a hot stove and remarks that I look tired. I try to slip away; and after a few minutes alone before my mirror, I can return looking cool, fresh, and rested, thanking God for the miracles of makeup.

Eveyone needs to be appreciated, encouraged, and loved. We were taught to follow and adjust to our husbands. Mother also told us, with a twinkle in her eye, there sometimes comes a time to stop submitting and start outwitting. Love and open physical affection were taught to us by example. I still remember when my grandparents were in their seventies, seeing them driving along the freeway holding hands. Or watching as my grandfather left to do some errands, kissing my grandmother like a young lover. Simple courtesy and thoughtfulness were exemplified also. Always asking what one could do for another was a way of life not just an exception. My mother has often said that she believes many marriage tensions would be absolved if each couple would take just five minutes a day and pray uniquely for the other one's needs. This helps us to concentrate on the needs of each other instead of just our own, and helps us to be less selfish and self-centered in the marriage relationship.

Marriage Is a Commitment

We were taught by word and examples that marriage was a lifelong commitment and not just a selfish, self-gratifying convenience; even though at times we all wondered if we had made a mistake, even Mother. When Mother was first married, she lived with her parents in the beautiful mountains of North Carolina. Daddy came up to the Chicago area and, without consulting Mother, accepted the pastorate of a church in Western Springs. Well, he wrote Mother a letter and told her that he had accepted this church. She was to move up, as he had already picked out the apartment, and it was just a lovely apartment. Well, she arrived, heartbroken to leave the mountains of North Carolina, and found that it was not a lovely apartment, but a dingy, dingy apartment on the railroad tracks. Talk about depression! Mother got so depressed that she put red cellophane on the wall and made it look like a fireplace where she could sit and read. And she hated the long cold winters of Chicago.

One day Daddy and some of his fellow workers

were going into Chicago and Mother said, "Look, Billy, please can I just go along? I won't stick with you, I just want to go window-shopping. You leave me in Chicago on one of the streets and I'll window-shop and you can pick me up later."

Daddy said, "Nope, nothing doing. We're going by ourselves. Our minds are made up and we won't take you with us."

Mother said, "Oh, please, just let me go with you."

"Nope, absolutely not," and Daddy closed the door and went out.

Mother burst into tears and she went in by her bed and got on her knees and said, "Lord, if you'll forgive me for marrying Billy, I promise I'll never do it again!"

Now she says she'd rather have a little bit of Daddy than a whole lot of anybody else. But the marriages I saw were full of being kind, one to another, tenderhearted, forgiving one another, "even as God for Christ's sake has forgiven you." The late Robert Quillan described marriage as "the union of two good forgivers."

If only we could realize how much God loves us unlovable creatures, that it is His very nature to love. God *is* love. Then, perhaps, we would begin to allow His nature to flow through and work in us so that we can love just a little bit like He loves. Because, you know, love blesses and helps, not only the one being loved, but also the one doing the loving. Someone once said, "Where we fail to be loving, we fail to be kind." Saint Teresa has said, "The true proficiency of the soul consists in much and warm loving." There's a little poem that Amy Carmichael has in one of her books that I think is especially good for mothers and for wives, too:

> I ask Thee for a selfless love,
> Through constant watchings wise,
> And a heart at leisure from itself
> To soothe and sympathize.

I think that's so beautiful. If we could just ask for a selfless love, then we could see all the little things we could do for our husbands and our children.

Photograph opposite: Gigi and her father leaving the church after her marriage.

The Old Couple

Thank you, Lord, for the old couple. I have known them all of my life, and have watched them growing old together. It has been beautiful and a very special blessing and joy for me. They have lived most of their lives, and are now ending them together as happy and as in love as when they first began. Thank you, Lord, for allowing me the privilege of living near them, for allowing me the moments that I shared with them, for allowing me to share in their love. To see them holding hands in the car as they drove along the freeway; for the times I saw him come in and bend over her pain-ridden body and look into her tired, yet loving eyes that always had a special gleam when he was around; and like a young lover, he would gently kiss her lips and ask, "How is my sweetheart today?"

Thank you for the example they are to young lovers, for the way he gently cares for her in her pain

Photograph opposite: Dr. and Mrs. L. Nelson Bell,
the author's maternal grandparents.

even though he himself is not well, for the wonderful way he understands her needs even without the spoken word, for how sweetly he reacts with tenderness or a joke when, because of her pain, she may be a bit cross. Thank you for her, for her devotion and love for him, for the faithful way she has followed and cared for him even when times were difficult and for the sweet oneness they have that makes it so she will allow no other to care for her. But, most of all, thank you for their love and their devotion to you, which is an inspiration to all. Thank you for allowing me to be their granddaughter; for through them, I have seen real love.

Gigi Graham Tchividjian

Father, before I close my eyes,
I would look back over the day
to see if I have used it well.
Whatever came, did I turn it to good?
Whatever opportunity arose,
did I see it as service to Thee?

If my answer is yes,
that is the praise of joyful lips;
but if uncertainty clothes my mind,
let it become readiness to greet the morrow
and serve Thee better,
so during the night watches
my meditation shall be sweet.

Author Unknown

Home Provides Direction

When I asked my thirteen-year-old what a home was, he answered, "A home is a place where we find direction." We found this in our home. When we were very young, my mother and daddy made all our decisions for us with our best in mind. Then, as we grew a little older, we learned to make these decisions together. My husband once said that he felt that it was very important to teach our children to listen to their own consciences because if we, as parents, continue to make all their decisions for them, pretty soon their consciences become lazy. My parents were very strong on all the moral issues, such as honesty, purity, respect of elders; but minor things that came as we were growing up, such as length of hair, or our choice in clothing, were never made issues. They stuck to all the important moral issues. They respected our individuality and our privacy. My parents never entered my bedroom without knocking, they never read my letters, even those from boyfriends, they never opened my diary, they never listened to our conversations on the telphone. They treated us with respect.

There were five of us and we were each very, very different. I remember one of my brothers went through a time when he loved rock music, at least to Mother it was rock. So Mother made a deal with him. She said, "All right, Franklin, I'll tell you what. You can listen to your rock music, but in your bedroom with the door closed. Please don't have it blaring all over the house."

Mother left, and a little bit later she came back with thirty missionaries for tea. She opened the front door; and what greeted her but this rock music blaring all over the house. She was furious, so she went flying up the stairs, two at a time, and my brother wasn't even in his room. He had just left his door open, the record on and blaring away, and he had left. So Mother took all his records. That night her conscience started to bother her, and the next day she went into Asheville and bought his favorite album. She came home and gave it to him and then she sat down on his bed and listened to it with him. Then they discussed it. That's communication. We were always free to talk to our parents about anything and we were always permitted to respectfully disagree. In fact, often they would admit they had been wrong. I have this saying above my desk.

It says, "Lord, when we are wrong, make us willing to change; and when we are right make us easy to live with."

Communication Takes Time

Recently, in a national magazine, I read that until now no one has found anything better for children than parents. Another recent article on the family said, "There is no better invention than the family, no better substitute." I believe that all of this takes time. Nothing replaces time together in a family. There is no way we can have real communication in our families today, in this complex society in which we live, if we do not take time. Some say that it is quality and not quantity that matters. In today's world, I'm not sure that I agree with that. I don't believe anything replaces time together, time to talk, time to disagree, to share, to love, to really get to know one another, to really know what's hurting my sister, what's hurting my mother, what's really bugging Dad, why is my husband upset today? Time just to be there, time to be available. Time to catch the first little signs or clues that something is wrong so that you can work together before it becomes a major problem.

My mother was always home. She sacrificed traveling, speaking, teaching, etc., and most of all being with Daddy, to be there with us, to be available. There were times when she must have wondered if it was worth it. But because I know how important it was for me growing up, I have done the same. I have wondered if it was worth it at times. I have asked myself, "Why do you make those homemade cookies from scratch when the kids would be just as happy with store-bought ones," or, "Why do you continue to clean little boys' rooms and bathrooms, when they seem to be just as content living in a mess?" The results of self-sacrifice for a mother are often not seen for many years. Often the recognition for hard labor is passed up or goes unnoticed or seemingly unappreciated. But the wages and the rewards are there, or will be. It is worth it all when your ten-year-old tells you that he likes having you at home when he returns from school, and that he wouldn't look forward to coming home if Mother were not there. That he likes running in to tell of all the day's activities, all the seemingly unimportant little incidences. My parents always had time when I was small. I don't remember ever going to my father's office and being told that he was too busy. He dropped everything for me. He made me feel important, significant, loved.

We all work at whatever we value. My husband and I value our relationship with our children and we value our relationship together. We have had to work at finding time to be together and we've had to give up other things but it's been worth it. Some young people might have to give up a date now and

Photograph opposite: The author's two oldest children in Switzerland.

then, or perhaps they might have to give up a school activity. A parent might have to give up a hobby, a dad might have to give up a promotion even, but it all depends on where our values are.

There are many practical ways of spending time together without making big or special plans. A daughter can help her mother do the dishes. A whole family can work together in the yard. When we lived up north, raking leaves wasn't one of our favorite jobs, but we made it a fun, family time. Making large piles, then jumping from a tree into the pile is fun. Putting a few twigs in with the leaves made a wonderful fire for roasting hot dogs and marshmallows and for taking the chill off as the fall air got cooler toward late afternoon. A father can take the oldest son with him as he goes to the bank or runs errands. I can't think of a place I would have rather been when I was young than home. And I am so thrilled that my husband and our children feel the same way.

Some people use television as a babysitter, or worse, a substitute parent. Others condemn it completely. But I think that even television can be a tool of communication and a family time together. We often sit together and watch a program. We do try to choose our programs. But this affords a wonderful opportunity to discuss together what we have watched, why certain things were wrong, or why others were right.

Photograph opposite: The Tchividjian children during a moment of play.

Photograph above: Gigi and Stephan Tchividjian
finding time to be alone, talking and
sharing together.

Together

Couples also need time alone. My husband is my best friend; we spend hours talking and sharing together. We have worked at this; and we have made it a priority in our relationship. We all work at what we value. Some of my friends work hard at tennis, others at golf, others at art or charities; all these things are fine, but it depends on what you value. My husband and I really value our relationship with each other so we have had to work at finding time to be together. We've had to give up other things to provide this time, but it's been worth it.

Because of this time together, my mind has been enlarged greatly. My husband has taught me so much and has brought so much into my life from his background and wide experience. When we disagree, we spend time talking it over; and we try never to make a major decision until we are in agreement. The greatest gift my husband has given to me after his love and total commitment, has been his gift of time.

Take Vacations Alone

Every couple should find time to take "vacations" together. Now, for some, this can be beautiful, expensive trips each year, for others, just a week-end or night at a hotel nearby. Maybe even a trip alone, camping or sending the kids to friends for the night. The important thing is to be together and to be alone. Alone to love, alone to talk, alone to reminisce, alone to make future plans and goals. Now some husbands are not aware that their wives would like to have time alone with them. Simply making them aware by discussing it can be very helpful. Sometimes Stephan or I will just mention to the other how much we long just to be alone for a weekend or an evening or even a walk, and you would be surprised at how good it makes one of us feel just to know that the other one wants to be together too.

If you have a husband who doesn't seem to need or want to take time out to be alone with you, then you need to ask yourself the question, why? Then see if there is anything that you can do to remedy the situation, anything that you can do to make him seek time to be with you. Here it is your responsibility to do all that is in your power to be the kind of person that he enjoys being with. For example, I

Photograph opposite: Ruth and Billy Graham on the porch of their home.

have a friend whose husband is a real estate lawyer. He needed someone to discuss his cases with, and she decided that someone might as well be herself. So she took courses and obtained her real estate license. She did what was in her power to make herself more attractive to him as a companion and helpmeet. Now that both of her children are in school, she has even gone back to work for her husband at his request.

My husband decided to go back to school, after being in business for many years, to obtain his doctorate in psychology. We had four small children, lived in a small apartment; so time alone was not easily come by. So that I could spend more time with him, I arranged my schedule to take a couple of courses with him. We had fun together, and I was able to add a few credits toward earning my college degree.

For Every Woman

For some, these examples would be impractical or impossible, but every woman can read an interesting book and learn to discuss it intelligently with her husband. Or every woman can watch the news once a day or read the newspaper to keep up with current events to make herself more interesting. It is a false concept to think that the only part of a woman that interests a man is physical. The secret to charm is being more interested in him than in

Photograph opposite: The author, Gigi Graham Tchividjian.

yourself. The physical is important, and we should do our very best to look as charming and as pretty as we can. But my mother once did a survey among some of her male acquaintances. She asked them if they could choose, which would they prefer, scenery or atmosphere? The single men said that atmosphere would be nice but they would prefer scenery. But without exception, the married men all said that they preferred atmosphere. The Bible says that "it is better to live on a corner of the roof, than share a house with a quarrelsome wife" (Prov. 21:9 N.I.V.). Atmosphere is important. And Proverbs 12:4 says, "A wife of noble character is her husband's crown, but a disgraceful wife is decay in his bones" (N.I.V.); and Proverbs 11:16 says, "A kindhearted woman gains respect" (N.I.V.). Someone once said, "The simplest way to express love is in simple deeds of kindness."

With Eternity's Values

In our busy, changing society, sometimes it is the wife who is too busy to be available. If this is the case, then I would suggest a real heart-searching time alone to see if your priorities and values are in order. With eternity's values in mind, list your activities and see where you have allowed just plain busyness to crowd out the more important things in life. Proverbs 31:16 in the Amplified version says, "She considers a new field [of interest or activity]

Photograph opposite: The author's sixth child.

before she buys or accepts it. Expanding prudently and not courting neglect of her present duties by assuming others. With her savings of time and strength she plants fruitful vines in her vineyards." I really think you will find that it is worth it to one day wake up and find fruit on the vine you planted, perhaps years ago, in your little vineyard.

Today there are so many options open to women. Some good, many valid options, but also many that bring confusion, and many questions. To marry or to remain single, to have a career or not, to bear children or not. And, for today's woman, each question must be thoughtfully considered and answered. I chose to ignore all those options, because, for as far back as I can remember, I just wanted to get married and have many children. The Lord tells us in the Bible that He shall give us our heart's desire if we delight ourselves in Him (Ps. 37:4). Even though I so often failed Him, He knew my inner being was just bursting to please Him, so He gave me my heart's desire and, at the age of seventeen, I married a man my father had chosen for me at fourteen, and I now have six children. On our fourteenth wedding anniversary, my little girl said, "You have been married fourteen years and only have five children? Boy, you had nine years to rest!" Well, not long after that, number six was born—our second little girl.

Thy Word Is Like a Garden, Lord

Thy Word is like a garden, Lord, with flowers
    bright and fair,
And everyone who seeks may pluck a lovely
    cluster there.
Thy Word is like a deep, deep mine, and jewels
    rich and rare
Are hidden in its mighty depths for every
    searcher there.

Thy Word is like a starry host: A thousand
    rays of light
Are seen to guide the traveler, and make his
    pathway bright.
Thy Word is like an armory, where soldiers
    may repair,
And find, for life's long battle day, all needful
    weapons there.

Oh, may I love Thy precious Word, may I
    explore the mine,
May I its fragrant flowers glean, may light
    upon me shine.
Oh, may I find my armor there, Thy Word my
    trusty sword;
I'll learn to fight with every foe the battle
    of the Lord.

Edwin Hodder

A Firm Foundation

Getting married to God's choice for me and having a large family was the only desire I have ever had, but still, obviously, I had to make the decision. I made it at a very early age, and with much counsel from my parents. I have never regretted the decision to continue my godly heritage.

I believe marriage to be a lifelong commitment, and Stephan and I entered marriage with this firm conviction. That doesn't mean it has all been easy; but our marriage started off on a firm foundation.

Ever since I was a very small girl, Mother and Daddy taught me to pray for my future life's partner. They explained to me that the boy that I was going to marry some day was approximately my age and that somewhere in the world he was going through similar problems and struggles. Because I followed my parents' teaching and prayed for my future husband, it never occurred to me that I wouldn't marry or that I might miss the right one when he came along. Then, too, I only dated Christian boys and never dated, what I called seriously, a boy that didn't have at least the characteristics of a man I would be willing to marry. I also told the Lord a strange thing. I told Him that I would not marry anyone until my entire immediate family agreed. Because I had a Christian family, and because I valued my godly heritage, I firmly believed that "the same Spirit says the same thing." In fact, that sentence is inscribed in our wedding bands.

Misunderstandings Will Occur

But, even starting out on as solid a foundation as we did, we have still had our share of ups and downs, and struggles of adjustments, too. Stephan is from an Oriental-European background and I from my small Southern town in the United States. When we were first married, there were many cultural shocks and hurdles to overcome. We were married in Switzerland and made our home there. I didn't speak a word of French at the time, and with family and friends thousands of miles away, it wasn't long before I became quite homesick. Tensions would build up, background differences had to be worked out, and a few heated arguments soon arose. We lived in a house on the side of a mountain overlooking the Swiss Alps. A very romantic setting, especially when the full moon would slide up from behind the mountains and shine down on our

Photograph opposite: The mountains surrounding the family home in Montreat, N.C.

little valley. But even this lovely fairy-tale setting with all its beauty could not make two such different persons, from such completely different backgrounds adjust without some difficulty.

I am one of those people who takes the verse Ephesians 4:26 at face value, and I don't like to let the sun go down upon my wrath. I like to settle things before I go to sleep at night, even if it means waking Stephan up at night to finish a fight. When we first married, Stephan had this thing that he would like to get away and cool off after, or worse yet, during an argument. This would infuriate me because he would leave me alone with my anger and with the kids. Well, at the time, we only had one car and he would go after those car keys. I remember quite vividly one such argument we were having in our bedroom overlooking those lovely, serene Swiss alps, when I looked in his eyes and saw right away that he was going after those car keys. This time I got to them first. We lived on the side of a mountain and had a balcony. I went to the window, onto that balcony, and I threw those car keys as hard and as far as I could; and we never found them.

Nietzsche once said, "He who has a why to live can bear with almost any how." There will be lots of ups and downs in a marriage, even one built on a foundation as firm as was ours, but when the "why" is to glorify God, then it makes the "hows" easier to handle.

Photograph opposite: Gigi with her newborn baby.

Happy is the family whose members
play together and work together
and know one another's hearts.

They think differently,
but their thoughts meet with understanding.
They follow different ways,
but their actions have a common purpose.

The unities of such a family
are like silken threads,
strong and true,
and woven together harmoniously.

Author Unknown

O Lord, bestow your blessing on
The children of this earth,
And let their lives be magic songs
Of merriment and mirth.
Protect them from the struggles and
The cares of older years.
Let not their bodies suffer or
Their eyes be filled with tears.
Show them the beauty of the world,
And help them understand
The need for love and virtue and
A warm and friendly hand.
O Lord, inspire them to grow
In goodness and in grace
And in the wisdom to attain
A more deserving place.
From time to time reveal to them
Reality and truth,
But let them laugh at foolish fears
And always keep their youth.

James J. Metcalfe

Ministries for Women

Recently, I was told wistfully by a housewife, "I wish that I had a ministry." I shared with her, as I will share with you, that I consider my home my God-given ministry. In 1 Timothy 5:14 we read, "I will, therefore, that the younger women marry, bear children and rule the house." And in Titus 2 we read that we are to love our husbands, love our children, and be the keepers at home. I find that I have a multitude of opportunities to minister. Now, I admit, that I don't always take them, but they are there right under my nose. If I am honest with myself, I will usually have to admit that the reason that I don't see them is because I am very often preoccupied with self. But then I ask the Lord once again for His selfless love, and take another look around, and there I find countless opportunities to minister.

I find as a homemaker that I have three basic ministries. First, I have a ministry to my man. In

Genesis we read that we were created to be help-meets; and Proverbs 31 deals more in detail about what kind of a helpmeet we are to be. Now this will mean something different to each woman because each man needs a different kind of a wife. There are no formulas for a happy marriage. That would be very nice, but it just isn't that easy. There are many wonderful principles and many good practical suggestions, but no set formulas. Each man's needs are different. Each family situation different, but everyone has the need to be loved, to be appreciated, needed, and encouraged.

A Ministry to My Man

Before I married, I was told by a dear Christian woman with six children, that I could ask for nothing more than a Christian gentleman for a husband. And that is exactly what the Lord gave me. If you have this kind of a man, don't take him for granted. But perhaps for one reason or another, you have a difficult marriage. Perhaps your husband is an alcoholic, or a wanderer, or perhaps just plain unappreciative. Well, Mother often told us that she thought that it was our job as wives to make our husbands happy, and that it was God's job to make them good. Disraeli's wife was a much older woman, very wealthy, and quite unattractive. In writing a book about her husband, she said, "Dizzy married me for money, but if he had to do it over again, he would marry me for love." She didn't try to make him good, only as happy as she could, and she was rewarded.

Some Things Only Christ Can Do

Another aspect of our ministry to our man is not to expect from our husbands what only Jesus Christ can be to us. Only Christ can totally satisfy, totally fulfill our needs and be everything to us. In fact, no other person or anything can be to you what God wants only His Son Jesus Christ to be. Our husbands are human; and I so often forget this and expect Stephan to do for me what I should be allowing Christ to do. Part of being a helpmeet is realizing that our husbands have needs, too, and looking for ways to satisfy and fulfill them instead of always expecting them to be there constantly fulfilling ours. For women married to difficult men, this can be a pretty lonely situation because you seem to always be on the giving end, but the alternatives are pretty grim, and the rewards of allowing Christ to be all in all are tremendous. Allowing Him to give peace where there is no peace, allowing Him to supply the strength when we are drained, allowing Him to give us His courage when we are defeated.

"If loving hearts were never lonely,
if all they wish might
always be,

> Accepting what they look for only,
> They might be glad, but not
> in Thee."

A. L. Waring

A Ministry to My Children

The second ministry that I have as a home-maker is to my children. Psalm 1:3 reads, "And he (or she) shall be like a tree, planted by the rivers of water, that bringeth forth its fruit in its season." One day the Lord spoke to me quite clearly in my heart and confirmed to me that my fruit-bearing season for now was at home with the children. After a Sunday service, one of America's well-known pastors was approached by a mother with a string of little children behind her. She told this minister that she felt that God was calling her to "minister." This pastor turned and gently but firmly, pointing to her children, said, "Yes, and there is your congregation." I was also taught the importance of ministering to the children by my mother. During our formative, growing up years, she took care of us almost exclusively. She didn't even teach a Bible study. As we left home and went out to begin lives and families of our own, she slowly began to add to and broaden this ministry. But, even now, if one of us children or one of her grandchildren needs her, she cancels whatever she had planned and comes and meets that need.

It is never too early, nor is it ever too late, to

Photograph opposite: The confirmation of the author's oldest son in Milwaukee, Wisconsin.

begin to minister to your children. Jochebed and
Hannah are two women in the Bible who have often
been an encouragement to me. Jochebed was the
mother of Moses, and Hannah was the mother of
Samuel. Both of these dear women only had their
little boys until they were weaned, which in those
days meant, perhaps, four or five years. Then Moses
was sent to the immoral and affluent Egyptian
court, and Samuel was sent to the temple to be
trained and raised by a priest named Eli, who had
not been able to raise or train his own boys. Both of
these young boys grew up under worldly and heathen
influences. Yet because of the early training from
their mothers, they both grew to be men of God. The
Scriptures say, "Train up a child in the way in
which he should go, and when he is old he will not
depart from it." My mother once said that the verse
reads "when he is old," not "when he is a teenager." I
firmly believe the Bible teaches that if a child is
given to the Lord even before birth, that God is
faithful and will bring that child back to Himself.
Even if for awhile that child may stray from his
early teaching. My husband's grandmother prayed
faithfully for my father-in-law for over forty years,
but she was rewarded and saw the fruits of her
labor. Now, because of her uncompromising faithfulness to the Lord, my husband's father and all of
his family are living for the Lord.

Perhaps for different reasons, you have not

been able to begin this early training of your children in the Lord. Perhaps you didn't know the Lord. For whatever reason you may have, perhaps this little illustration will help you. Some time ago in England, there was a group of friends that met in a pub after a hunt. They were talking and sharing the day's activities. One hunter, quite excited, began to relate his story using quite a few gestures. All of a sudden, with one such gesture, he hit a cup of tea and knocked it all over the beautifully whitewashed walls. He was terribly embarrassed, but before he could even apologize, one of the other men jumped to his feet and, pulling a pen from his pocket, began to sketch on the wall. As he sketched, there emerged the most magnificent, majestic stag. That man was Landseer, England's foremost painter of animals. I believe, that if Landseer can do that with an ugly brown tea stain, how much more can God make something beautiful out of all our faults and all our failures if we will just give them to Him and allow Him to sketch and work as He sees fit; and we being available, but not getting in His way.

God Sees Beyond

My mother told the story of a man she met once, an interesting character, who was an archeologist with a passion for old china. Most of us don't have much patience for old, broken china, and it usually gets put out with the trash. To this man, it was a challenge. In fact, he had built a home that was a monstrosity out of all the old, broken odd things he could find, and to him his home was beautiful. He had also sifted through all the dirt around his house and collected all the bits and pieces of pottery and china, and then he spent hours patiently, carefully, gluing them back together. My mother asked if she could have one of his carefully glued pieces of pottery, but she asked for one that didn't have all the pieces. He looked at my mother a bit strangely because of her request. She then explained why she wanted one of his plates or vases, "You remind me of God," she said, "Because God so carefully and lovingly takes the broken pieces of our lives and puts them back together again. But,here and there, there is a piece missing; someone has died, there has been a divorce; somewhere we have made a mistake, and a piece is missing. But God lovingly glues us back together." I love that story, because I believe it applies to all of us. We all have cracks, if not big pieces, missing.We all have hurts of disappointments that we have to learn to allow God to handle and put back into place. We can go on without those pieces if the glue is strong; and one day, in eternity, all those broken pieces will find their places, and we will stand perfect before Him. He sees beyond our faults; He sees our needs.

Perhaps, you are concerned about your children or even the children of someone else. *Time* magazine

Photograph opposite: The author's oldest son with his grandparents, Ruth and Billy Graham.

once quoted Andrew Wyeth, the great American artist, as saying, "The most irritating experience an artist can have is to have his work criticized before it is finished." We often do just that with God's work before it is finished.

My father, being away so much of the time, left much of the raising and education to my mother. In an interview, she was once asked how she had done it? She replied very simply, "On my knees." We can all do that; children of all ages can be raised on our knees.

What a privilege to have been raised by a mother and a father who spent so much of their time on their knees for us. Now I falteringly try to follow their example. Just before the birth of my second child, my mother sent me the following poem as a Mother's Day gift.

To Gigi by Ruth Bell Graham

It seems but yesterday
you lay
new in my arms.
Into our lives you brought
sunshine
and laughter
play—
showers, too,
and song.

Headstrong,
heartstrong,
gay,
tender beyond believing,
simple in faith,
clear-eyed,
shy,
eager for life—
you left us
rich in memories,
little wife.
And now today
I hear you say
words wise beyond your years;
I watch you play
with your small son,
tenderest of mothers.
Years slip away—
today
we are mothers
together.

From *Sitting by My Laughing Fire* . . . by Ruth Bell Graham.
Copyright © 1977 by Ruth Bell Graham. Used by permission of the
author and Word Books, Publisher, Waco, Texas 76703.

A Ministry to My Community

The third basic ministry that I find I have is to my
community. Any woman who wishes to have a
ministry outside her home just has to take a few
moments to stop and think, and I am sure it won't be

long before many things will come to mind that she could do. If there are any elderly or lonely persons in your area, perhaps a card or a visit, or sending a child to visit with a nice warm loaf of home-baked bread or cake would be a blessing, not only to the person being visited, but also to the child. My older children went once a week with friends from their school to visit persons in a nursing home. This turned into a multiple blessing. The children realized anew the value of old age and began to have a better love and respect for the elderly. The persons in the home lit up when they saw the children arriving.

Is there any trash on your streets? Perhaps a family "doing," could be to take a walk together and pick up the trash as you go. You combine teaching your children, spending time with them, ministering to them, and ministering to your community all at the same time.

Tending Our Own Garden

Many of our larger communities are very transient and so lack stability and roots; they are ever in motion within as well as without. Many women I talk with find it difficult to make lasting friends and so are afraid to get involved with others, afraid of being hurt, and so they are lonely. Perhaps your ministry could be being a friend. My husband, in his work as a psychologist, has a group of women from a church who are willing to be called on just to be

ograph above: Two of the Tchividjian children
g for Dad.

friends. For example, if someone is going through a divorce, or has a problem with a teenager, or has experienced illness or death in her family, this group of women can be called on to minister to the one hurting. Go have lunch with her, or go shopping with her, or perhaps take her children for the day or even a night or two so that she can be alone with her husband. These are all examples of ministering to our community. But, the best way to minister to our communities is to be an example by tending our own gardens well, by being a sweet smelling savor. Does your garden invite inquiries as to why and how it is so pleasing? My mother tells a story about me to prove this point. When we were all quite small, one morning before school, Mother jumped out of bed, threw on a robe and slippers, didn't even have time to comb her hair, grabbed my little brother from his crib, lacking the time to change his diapers, and rushed into the kitchen to prepare our breakfast. My sister Bunny came downstairs in a very jovial mood, and was happily talking a blue streak. I have always been slow to get going in the morning and need a little time to get my blood circulating to the point where I am even civil. Well, I arrived on this scene and sat down to eat my breakfast. After a few moments, I had had enough. I threw down my fork, pushed my chair back, stood up, and said, "Mother, between looking at you, smelling Franklin, and listening to Bunny, I am just not hungry." Is this the way your community feels about your family? I am afraid that my family is often unappetizing. With six children there is quite a bit of noise, and not all of it is pleasant. Once, a motel was enlarging, and there was this sign in the lobby, "Sorry for the noise and inconvenience, but we are growing." I have often thought about having that sign printed for my yard. I don't think we have to be a blessing, but we do have to be real.

These ministries, to my husband, my children, and my community are the three basic ministries in my life now. But they include so many things, and we don't always see immediate results to our labors.

The work we do today needs doing again tomorrow. The same floor we cleaned today is dirty again a few hours later; the same clothes need washing and rewashing; the dinner we slaved over for several hours is devoured in minutes; the remarks we made yesterday need restating and reminding today. We don't receive promotions nor raises in order to better evaluate our job. Many years of reminding, disciplining, schooling, loving, encouraging pass before we begin to see the fruits of our labor. But if we take the time to notice, there are daily wages. The little dirty kiss planted on our cheek for no apparent reason, the unexpected "thank you" from our teenager. The sheer pleasure of seeing the image of God in a growing child, to hear the first small attempts to pray alone as they begin to grow in the knowledge of God.

Discouragement Will Come

With a husband and six children, I find that I have a household that never stops; and I must admit, there are times that I get a bit discouraged and tired. Not from lack of love and appreciation, but from the fact that every minute is taken and busy. A verse taken from a translation by William F. Beck has blessed me.

Lord, the rivers make a noise,
the rivers make a roaring noise,
the rivers make a crashing noise,
But, more than the noise is
the might of the Lord above.

This thought has blessed me because I can find quiet amid the noise if I remember my resources which are all wrapped up in the person of Jesus Christ. He can give quiet amid the storm; He can give strength when I feel I am at the end of mine. He never promised to take away all hardship, all sorrow, nor absolve all impossible situations, nor remove all the giants in our lives; but He did and does promise to be with us in and through these times and for all time.

Who Notices? God

I remember one day that I was especially tired. I had scrubbed and cleaned all day, taken care of the kids, including a baby that required a lot of attention and would let me know of her feeling or lack of it by the overuse of her lungs. I remember that I was cleaning the bathtub in my teenage boys' room, when I had just about all I could take. I sat down on the floor, and the tears began to trickle down my cheek. I asked myself and the Lord if it were really worth it all. There, on the floor beside that tub, that probably no one would notice was clean or not, I heard a voice in my heart say so very clearly, "Inasmuch as ye have done it unto one of the least of these, ye have done it unto me" (Matt. 25:40). A sweet quiet came over me as I realized anew my resource and that all that I did for those I loved, I was also doing for Him. Each necessary menial task He was noticing and He was there right beside me. That made all the difference in my attitude. I got up, and dried my tears with a renewal of spirit.

Praise and Pray

When I was young we used to have a very practical little saying: "Discouragement is the devil's calling card." So when we are discouraged, we know that the devil has been around and we must quickly turn our eyes away from self and return to our resource of strength. Another little saying that was always in our kitchen when I was growing up and now is in my kitchen says, "Praise and Pray and Peg away." I find that the attitude of praise has a lot to do with helping me get through particularly difficult days.

Praise Him in All Things

Not long after I was married, we went to live in a country that lacked many of the modern conveniences to which I had been accustomed. I had a little baby and there were no paper diapers. I also had no washing machine, and so we had a very large pot that we put on the stove after breakfast each morning and boiled all the baby's clothes. We also washed the sheets in the bathtub. I remember my mother lovingly writing to me at this time and telling me how grateful she was that I had diapers to wash, a baby who needed diapers, hands with which to scrub, and soap with which to wash. That sounds a bit tough, perhaps, but it made me even more grateful for all that I had; and so I could praise my heavenly Father all the more. I also praised Him for such a loving, caring Mother. It is not always the big things that get to us. It is more often an accumulation of small things. I remember once again such a time in my life when so many small insignificant things were piling up to the point that I was again asking if it was really worth it all. My mother knew nothing of my feelings, and I was thousands of miles away from her, but the Lord knew. One day I opened my mail and found this poem from my mother, written especially for me.

Photograph opposite: The author's husband, Stephan, with their baby.

To Gigi from Ruth Bell Graham

The little things that bug me,
resentments deep within;
the things I ought to do, undone,
the irritations one by one
till nerves stretch screaming-thin
and bare for all the world to see—
which needs His touch to make it whole
the most, my body or my soul?

I pray—but nothing comes out right,
my thoughts go flying everywhere;
my attitudes are all confused,
I hate myself—I am not used
to hands all clenched, not clasped, in prayer
and heart too leaden to take flight;
which, oh, which needs to be whole
the most, my body or my soul?

I cannot read. I cannot pray.
I cannot even think.
Where to from here? and how get there
with only darkness everywhere?
I ought to rise and only sink . . .
and feel His arms, and hear Him say,
"I love you" . . . It was all my soul
or body needed to be whole.

Ruth Bell Graham

From *Sitting by My Laughing Fire* . . . by Ruth Bell Graham.
Copyright © 1977 by Ruth Bell Graham. Used by permission of the
author and Word Books, Publisher, Waco, Texas 76703.

Prayer Is the Soul's Sincere Desire

Prayer is the soul's sincere desire,
Unuttered or expressed,
The motion of a hidden fire
That trembles in the breast.

Prayer is the burden of a sigh,
The falling of a tear,
The upward glancing of an eye,
When none but God is near.

Prayer is the simplest form of speech
That infant lips can try.
Prayer, the sublimest strains that reach
The Majesty on high.

Prayer is the contrite sinner's voice
Returning from his ways,
While angels in their songs rejoice
And cry, "Behold, he prays."

Prayer is the Christian's vital breath,
The Christian's native air,
His watchword at the gates of death;
He enters heaven with prayer.

No prayer is made by man alone;
The Holy Spirit pleads,
And Jesus on the eternal throne
For sinners intercedes.

O Thou, by whom we come to God,
The Life, the Truth, the Way,
The path of prayer Thyself hast trod,
Lord, teach us how to pray.

James Montgomery

Fulfillment

Matthew 20:28 says that Christ came to minister, not to be ministered unto. I find that in order to minister in Christ's way, willing to serve, unselfishly, that I have little time to think of myself. I have found this to be very healthy. I learned this, too, from my family by example. I don't think that it ever occurred to either my parents or my grandparents to think of themselves first or even think of themselves much at all. A psychologist friend of ours says that the word "trapped" is a word that he would say describes the feelings of so many of his patients; and that he would define "trapped" as too often using the personal pronouns: I feel, I think, My life, Myself, etc. Often we are so terribly preoccupied with Self.

In the last few years, we have been inundated,

especially among women, with words like freedom, identity, fulfillment, self-assertion, etc. None of these concepts are bad in themselves; but when I find these words creeping into my mind ahead of the Lord Jesus Christ, or the responsibilities and ministries that He gave me to do, then I take care. I try to find a little time and once again take inward inventory (watch out for the devil's old trick "morbid introspection") of my priorities, goals, the real desires of my heart. Most of all, I must determine if these things are glorifying God and if they are fitting into His plan for my life. A good way to avoid morbid introspection and determine if your goals are good is expressed in these words:

> Turn your eyes upon Jesus,
> Look full in His wonderful face,
> And the things of earth will grow strangely dim,
> In the light of His Glory and Grace.

Who Am I?

Many of the women I see and talk to have been confused by the words freedom, identity, fulfillment, etc. and are seeking answers. Often their seeking leads them down one dead end after another.

Photograph opposite: Gigi's son's confirmation cake. Inscription reads: "I have no greater joy than to know that my children walk in truth" (3 John 1:4).

Some are seeking answers in a bottle of alcohol or tranquilizers, others are seeking fulfillment in an affair or trying to "find" themselves in the office of a psychiatrist. The world has little, if any, real answers for women today.

Women are also confused as to who they are; they are confused as to who and what they should be. They are confused as to where they are going; they have confused priorities and they have confused the issues. They are confused because of changing ideals, a lack of authority, and a lack of absolutes.

Freedom Is Many Things

Women have been demanding "freedom" but I don't believe that we are honest in our quest or with ourselves if we don't first ask, freedom from what and freedom for what? We can have all the freedom we want and demand all the legal freedom, all the sexual freedom, all the free time we desire, but, there is one problem: we are still stuck with ourselves.

It seems that first of all, we need freedom from ourselves. There are three basic freedoms that a woman needs to be truly free. One is that she needs a freedom from her past. There is no way that you can be totally free, completely free, if you are carrying around a burden of guilt, or perhaps some bad habits, some grave failures or even a sense of

Photograph opposite: The author's parents at their grandson's confirmation.

dissatisfaction with your past. Even though I accepted the Lord Jesus at four years old and asked Him to forgive my sins, and He did, I still need freedom from yesterday's failures, freedom from the burden of guilt that I carry when I yell at my children unnecessarily, for not being the type of woman my husband needed when he came home tired, for not being the thoughtful neighbor or loving friend, or perhaps just being too busy, too busy to even worship Him. I need freedom from those guilts and failures. We cannot go back and undo our past, but we can ask God to overrule all our mistakes. Only a knowledge and assurance of total forgiveness can free us from our past; and only the blood of our Lord Jesus Christ can do that.

A woman, to be really free, also needs freedom from or in her present, a freedom that comes from being controlled not by ourselves, and not by our compulsions or desires, but a freedom that comes from living a Spirit-controlled life. A life controlled by the Holy Spirit is true freedom. If our past has been forgiven and the Holy Spirit is controlling our present, then we can be free from our endlessness, free from our seeking, free from our searching, free from our boredom, or free from the barren times of business. If our hearts and our minds are free, then we can have freedom for the future, freedom to be what God wants and intends us to be. If we are free from ourselves, then we will have the freedom to minister, to worship, and to glorify God.

Fulfillment

Another word we see a lot in print and hear spoken often is the word fulfillment, or rather self-fulfillment, self-satisfaction. There is absolutely nothing wrong with seeking to better our minds or to find an occupation in order to use our time more wisely, but we must be careful of the motives.

I married at seventeen, so I never finished college. When we came back to the United States and my husband resumed his studies toward his doctorate, I felt some pressure to go back to college. I went back and took a few courses. I had three children and was pregnant with my fourth; I had no help at home; and my husband was a busy father and student. I was determined to make "A's," which I did, but I had to study hard, plus clean house, cook, and put up with morning sickness as well as continue to be a good wife and mother. One day, I asked myself what my motives were. I started out with right motives. I love to learn and to study; I wanted to increase my knowledge and not let my husband outgrow me; but, as time went on, a bit of pride crept in. People were patting me on the back and saying, "How do you do it all? How do you make "A's," take care of a home and children and even continue to look nice?" I began to like these questions. Now, I didn't drop my classes, but I did cut down and I did adjust my motives. (I still haven't finished college but still love to learn and, perhaps, one day I will finish college.) Dr. Larry Crabb, a psychologist, once said, "The real block to self-fulfillment is a preoccupation with self."

Psalm 17:15 says, "My contentment is in knowing all is well between us" (Living Bible). That's fulfillment; knowing that all is well between the Heavenly Father and us. We find fulfillment when we are filled with the Holy Spirit. We find fulfillment when we are doing what we were created to do. The Westminster catechism states that, "Man's chief end is to glorify God and to enjoy Him forever." That's fulfillment. We were created to glorify God and to enjoy Him forever.

The following passage by Armelle Nicolas is one I love and has helped me. I would like to share it with you:

"As soon as I woke in the morning I threw myself into the arms of Divine Love as a child does into its father's arms. I rose to serve Him, and to perform my daily labor simply that I might please Him. If I had time for prayer, I fell on my knees in His divine presence, consecrated myself to Him and begged Him that He would accomplish His holy will perfectly in me and through me and that He would not permit me to offend Him in the least thing all through the day. I occupied myself with Him and His praise as

Photograph opposite: Dr. Graham playing with his grandchild.

long as my duties permitted. Very often, I had not even the leisure to say a prayer during the day; but that did not trouble me. I thought it as much my duty to work for Him as to pray to Him, for He Himself had taught me, that all that I should do for love of Him would be true prayer. I loved Him and rejoiced in Him. If my occupations required all my attention, I had nevertheless my heart towards Him; and, as soon as they were finished, I ran to Him again, as to my dearest Friend. When evening fell and everyone went to rest, I found mine only in the Divine Love, and fell asleep, still loving and adoring Him."

Armelle Nicolas

True Fulfillment

Armelle Nicolas describes true fulfillment, being in fellowship and communion with the Father in all that we do and in whatever we do. To me this is real Christianity—not a religion but a life; and a way of life. In finding our fulfillment in the Father, we will also find our identity; because for a Christian our identity is Jesus Christ. Paul says in Philippians 1:21 that "For me to live is Christ," and John says in John 3:30, "He must increase and I must decrease." I am often asked, "Isn't it hard to be the daughter of a famous man?" or, "What is it like to be the daughter of such a famous person?" And to be honest, until now, this has never bothered me because it was

Photograph opposite: A proud and happy grandpa holding his grandson.

instilled in me from the time that I can remember that I was to seek my identity in the person of Jesus Christ. Anything else would be identity spelled with a capital "I." As Paul says in Galatians, it is no "longer I but Christ that liveth in me." Matthew 10:39 teaches a principle that the more we lose our lives, the more we will find them. This has been true in my life. The times in my life when I was preoccupied with myself, I soon found that the days were slipping by and I was losing and wasting them.

But each time He gently reminded me in a loving but firm way that this was not His will nor way for me; and I once again made the glory of God and the ministries that He gave me my preoccupation. Then, I once again began to know what real living was all about. Not just existing from day to day, but living each day to the fullest for Him.

Seeking identity outside of the person of Jesus Christ to me is just a simple ego trip; and Satan still has every trick that he used in the Garden of Eden with Eve and he's sharpened them, brought them up to date, and made them very accessible and attractive to us women to try to get us looking at ourselves instead of fixing our eyes on Jesus Christ. Satan can even use our ministries to do this. We can get so wrapped up in doing those tasks that the Lord Jesus gave to us in our way, that we forget to simply worship Him and show Him our utter devotion. There are times that we need simply to "Be still and know that He is God." His way of doing things always leaves room for worship and quiet devotion to Him.

Lord, Is All Well?

Lord, is all well? Oh, tell me; is all well?
No voice of man can reassure the soul
When over it the waves and billows roll;
His words are like the tinkling of a bell.
Do Thou speak; is all well?

Across the turmoil of wind and sea,
But as it seemed from somewhere near to me,
A voice I know—Child, look at Calvary;
By the merits of My Blood, all is well.

Whence came the voice? Lo, He is in the boat:
Lord, wert Thou resting in Thy love when I,
Faithless and fearful, broke into that cry?
O Lord, forgive; a shell would keep afloat
Didst Thou make it Thy boat.

And now I hear Thy mighty "Peace be still,"
And wind and wave are calm, their fury froth.
Could wind or wave cause Thee to break Thy troth?
They are but servants to thy sovereign will;
Within me all is still.

Oh was there ever light on land or sea,
Or ever sweetness of the morning air,
Or ever clear blue gladness anywhere
Like this that flows from Love on Calvary—
From Him who stilled the sea?
Father and Son and Spirit be adored:
Father who gave to death our Blessed Lord;
Spirit, who speaks through the Eternal Word
By the merits of the Blood, all is well.

Amy Carmichael

O Thou, the captain of my salvation,
Strengthen me inwardly and outwardly
That I may be vigorous with spiritual purpose
And disposed to every virtuous
  and gallant undertaking.
Grant that I may do valiantly
In despite of slothfulness or timidity.
And that neither my fear of ridicule
Nor my love of popularity
May make me seem to like what is not right.
Be Thou pleased also
To fortify my spirit
So that I may meet life hopefully
And be able to endure everything
Which Thou mayest be pleased to send me.

        Author Unknown

Abiding in Christ

As a child, I gave my heart to the Lord Jesus as Savior; then, as I continued to grow as a young woman and as a child of God, I became conscious that he was also my Lord. I also became conscious of the fact that deep down in my innermost being, my deepest and most sincere desire was to glorify Him in whatever I did. I also found myself failing so often, but being taught quite early that discouragement and despair are tools of Satan. The thing to do if we find we have failed is to acknowledge the failure, ask for forgiveness, then arise and go on. I also found that each time I failed, I would go back to my guidebook, my source of authority, the Bible, and see what He would have me to do as a woman trying to live for Him. I have had quite a few unpleasant experiences when I have purchased an item and failed to read the manufacturer's instructions because I am lazy, or in a hurry, or because I think I can figure it out all on my own. When the item doesn't work properly, or the blouse shrinks, I know who is to blame: me. So it is in my Christian walk and growth. When I fail, I run back to the book and once again read the instructions, because somewhere I had failed to follow them.

God's Word Is Plain

I have found the Bible to be so plain and so simple in its instructions; the principles are set forth clearly, and practical advice is abundant. Proverbs is filled with nuggets of wisdom for wives, mothers, and human relationships in general. The women of the Bible are numerous and their experiences and examples are varied and applicable today. Most of these women had homes and their problems weren't much different from ours. Perhaps circumstances and cultures have changed a bit, but human nature is the same. I have found the Word of God my greatest source of wisdom and strength in my quest to glorify God as a wife and mother.

There are many aspects to growing as a Christian, but I have found that they all come back to two that are essential: abiding and obedience.

Abiding

The Bible teaches, in John 15, the importance of abiding. If we are to grow, we must abide in the vine which is the person of Jesus Christ. We hear much about the fruit of the Spirit spoken of in Galatians 5:22 which is love, joy, peace, long-suffering, gentleness, goodness, faith, meekness, self-control; but we cannot have these if we are not abiding. Fruit has to be grown; it doesn't just appear overnight but rather takes hours, days, weeks, months, of abiding on the vine before it is ripe and beautiful and desirable.

Abiding in and putting on the person of Jesus Christ is an everyday, moment by moment, growing process. We abide by saturating ourselves with the Word of God, reading the Word. Each of us needs a special time each day to let God speak to us through His Word. I went to a Christian high school which taught the idea "no Bible, no breakfast," and I still believe that the principle of teaching good habits is so important. For some, the early morning hours are the best. My mother always got up before us children to have time with the Lord. I find the pressures of the day begin to crowd in on me as soon as I awake; and since I tend to be a night person, I prefer the closing of the day, after the kids are asleep, when the house is clean, and all is quiet. The important thing is to set aside a special time each day. I heard recently of "planned neglect." I had never heard of it before, but the idea is a good one. If you find that your days are too full, and the day is over and done, and you have had no time to spend alone with the Word of God, then you plan to neglect something else. You must make time to spend with the Lord. I have found that it makes a big difference in how I handle situations, the children, or even the mundane, everyday, ordinary things in my life.

Study God's Word

There are several ways to spend time with the Word of God. For instance, there is personal devotional reading and meditating. Taking the Bible, and asking God to speak to your heart as you read His Word, then spending a few moments meditating on what this means to you. Then there is personal study, when you take a portion of Scripture and a notebook, and a good commentary or reference book, and study the Bible in more depth. Some new Christians find this difficult and get a bit discouraged. It does take a bit of time to learn how to do this.

Sometimes I like to do word studies. For example, I will take a word such as *forgiveness* and look up all the references to that word in the Bible. Then I make notes and soon I have a pretty good idea what God says about forgiveness. There are also book studies, taking a certain book of the Bible and reading and studying it. Or subject studies, for example, how to know the will of God, or how to deal with our thoughts. I look up different words on the subject and their synonyms and then find references to these words in the Scripture, and soon I am making exciting discoveries.

Photograph opposite: The author's parents finding time to spend in the Word.

Another way to study the Scripture is to attend a Bible study, and a Bible teaching church. I find that I receive real strength in studying the Word of God as a group. Bible studies have become plentiful in the last few years, and this is a blessing we in America have that not much of the world shares. But there is also a danger here. I know many women that go from Bible study to Bible study, but rarely or never dig and glean on their own. They find it more pleasant to let someone else dig and then spoonfeed them. One does not replace the other. We need both the intimate time alone with the Word, and the "assembling of ourselves together" in order to worship and study.

Memorize God's Word

Another way of abiding in the Living Word is memorizing verses and even passages. One day we may not have the written Word, but it will be a lot more difficult to take away what we have hidden in our hearts and minds. I teach my children verses from the time they begin to talk, and it always amazes me how quickly their little minds grasp the words; but I personally find memorizing difficult. Memorizing, however, is a simple way of abiding in the Word all during the day, no matter how busy. Just place a much-loved Bible verse or passage in the kitchen, on the ironing board, or in your jacket pocket and take it out while waiting at the doctor's office or elsewhere. I even place a verse in the car and repeat it while driving or waiting in traffic. Memorized Scripture can comfort and strengthen. We had two friends that were on the other side of the world when they received word that their oldest son, his wife, and their infant grandchild had all been killed in an automobile accident. Later, those friends said that it was the Scripture they had put to memory that kept them from going crazy those first few weeks.

My paternal grandmother, who is eighty-seven years old, was recently in the hospital. I went to visit her, and she shared her experience when the doctor came to see her and tell her of her condition. After he had spoken, she was upset to the point of not being able to speak for a few moments. The doctor was momentarily called out of the room and instinctively she turned to her Lord, whom she had known for so many years, for comfort and strength. A Bible verse that she had put to memory many years before came to her mind and gave her the needed comfort and strength for her stay in the hospital. The Word of God is a living Word; it is the person of Jesus Christ Himself revealed to us. Psalm 119 says that the Word cleanses, strengthens, delights, teaches, saves, comforts, directs, gives understanding. These are just a few of the things the Word of God does in just one Psalm. What a resource!

I am so grateful that I was taught early to use

this resource. To draw strength from it, to use it in seeking direction and guidance, to use it in times of discouragement, disappointment, and loneliness. My mother had gone away to North Korea to high school at the age of thirteen and she suffered terribly from homesickness. There, all she had learned was put to the test; and it was there that the Living Word became a true resource from which she could draw. I also left home to go away to school at the age of twelve and I suffered terribly from that awful gnawing feeling in the pit of the stomach that comes from being lonely and homesick. But because I had been taught early to turn to the Lord and to His Word for strength and comfort, I now look back on those days as a spiritual experience for which I will be forever grateful. I learned many things during those weeks and months about the vast resource that I had in my personal relationship with the Lord Jesus and in His Word. Since those days as a very young girl there have been many disappointments, heartaches, times of decision, times of discouragement; and each time I have gone to His Word. He has never once failed me. I am so grateful that as a very young girl I learned His promises are for real.

God's Word Is the Authority

Not only was I taught early to draw upon the Word as a resource, but I was taught that as a Christian, the Word was my authority. This has

134

been a great source of strength and encouragement to me. The world in which we now live is getting more and more confusing, with less and less absolutes. More of the "do your own thing" or "if it feels good, do it" philosophy. There are times that I have questioned my values, but again, I am so thankful I have been taught to go and search out my own answers from the Word of God. This was especially important to me as a teenager. When my mind was filled with questions and my feelings were causing much confusion, I knew that I could rely on God's Word to straighten out my thoughts and feelings. Psalm 119:105 says, "Thy Word is a lamp unto my feet and a light unto my path." The following is a poem based on Psalm 119:18 that I wrote and put in the front of my Bible as a young teenager.

"Open my eyes that I may behold wondrous things out of Thy law."

Lord, open my eyes that I may see,
What You have today for me.
What I should learn, what I should do,
Starting my day looking to You.

Lord, open my eyes that I may see,
What You have in Your Word for me.
What I should read, what I should hear,
Starting with You my day is so dear.

Lord, open my eyes that I may see,
What You have in this prayer for me.
What I should feel, what I should say,
Praying with You begins my day.

Lord, open my eyes that I may see,
Each day, my opportunity
To win some sin-bound soul for Thee,
And in so doing, they may be free.

Lord, open my eyes all the way.
Open them wide and let them stay
Only on You till eternity.
Lord, this the only way for me.

Gigi Graham Tchividjian

Prayer

Another way in which we abide is through prayer. Prayer is simply talking to God. As soon as I could talk, I was taught to pray verbally and before I could talk, I was taught to pray by example. I was taught to pray about everything and anything. Nothing was too big or too small to talk to God about. I discovered very early the joys of answered prayer and have continued to rejoice as I become more and more conscious of the heights yet to be scaled in my prayer life. I believe that the soul's greatest need is communion with God, and prayer fulfills a great part of this need.

It is in prayer that we receive a better understanding of God. Often we look on prayer as a means of getting something for ourselves, but the idea of prayer as set forth in the Bible is that we may get to know God Himself in a more intimate way. Some say that "prayer changes things." This is true, but it is also true, and perhaps more important, that prayer changes the one praying. Prayer works wonders on our disposition. I have often experienced times of utter frustration as a mother of many young children of differing ages.

Morning in My Family

I find that it doesn't take much to make me cross. I remember one day last spring I awoke a little before seven in the morning after a night of several interruptions with a new baby in the room. I have always found it hard to get up in the morning; but I usually function pretty well after a couple of cups of coffee. My family has learned not to expect too much from me before the two cups have been downed. On this particular morning, I arrived downstairs in anticipation of the much-needed coffee. Before I even reached the kitchen, however, I heard the noise of a before school free-for-all in progress. I tried to gather some false strength and push my way to the coffee pot, but the two-year-old had spilled his orange juice and it needed cleaning. Just as that task was ending, the five-year-old spilled his. Before

Photograph above: Three of the author's children conducting a garage sale. This is only one of many ways she has found to encourage togetherness and sharing in the family, helping to create happy memories for her children.

139

the second clean-up could be completed, it was time for the four oldest children to leave the house for school. All of a sudden, the oldest remembered that he had not done his chores, nor had he gotten together his gym clothes. The five-year-old suddenly screamed, for no reason, then he hit the two-year-old. I spanked the five-year-old, and still no coffee. I turned to the oldest and yelled at him to get moving. The nine-year-old decided that this was a good time to keep things lively by stirring things up a little more. When I scolded him for this, he had the nerve to argue with me. And still no coffee. Then the oldest told me if having six kids was like this, he didn't want any and he'd like to know why I had had any. Hurt, I somehow managed to comb the different heads of hair, wash the breakfast off the faces, and see the children out the door to school. A bit late, I turned to grab the much-needed coffee and caught the two-year-old drinking the bottle of pancake syrup. Before I could get to him, he saw me and quickly turned the bottle upside down and poured the rest onto the carpet. I still had no coffee.

Perhaps this particular day I had reason to be cross and nervous; but often it takes much less to make me tense, and I take out this tension and frustration on the family. But I have found that a few moments alone on my knees in prayer and fellowship with my heavenly Father, who cares and understands, changes me and my disposition. There are times, such as the morning just described, when I don't have time to slip away. Here is where instant, spontaneous prayer comes in. The "O Lord, help me" prayers. And you know, He does help.

Pray Unceasingly

I remember one pastor saying the biggest problem with prayer is prayerlessness. This is so true. I have found it so in my own life, because prayer, disciplined and regular prayer, is an effort of the will. In my situation, I don't have much trouble with spontaneous prayer, nor with the attitude of praying without ceasing. I pray while driving, I pray while doing the laundry, or cooking, or cleaning. I pray as I tuck the children in bed, as I walk or sit in the garden. But to make the necessary effort of my will to pray in a regular, disciplined way, I fall short. Praying without ceasing is important and we are told to do so in Thessalonians 5:17, but developing a regular disciplined prayer life is also equally important. There is an old saying that I have always loved.

> "Satan trembles when he sees
> The weakest saint
> Upon his knees."

And because of this, Satan will do his best to distract and discourage us.

I have always been thankful to my Heavenly

Father for all that He has done for me; and I was taught early to verbally express my gratitude to Him. But it wasn't until recently, while studying the different aspects of prayer, that I really began to discover the importance of praise and adoration in prayer. I found that praise and adoration purges my prayers from the all too often selfishness that creeps in. I discover a new source of strength and courage when, in adoration, I take time to think of who He is and what He has done. In adoration, I bow before my Creator in total worship of Him. Harold Lindsell in his book entitled *When You Pray* says, "If adoration alone is engaged in, the aspiring soul needs nothing more. It has already found God, and that is enough."

I have always been a good repenter. Perhaps God made me this way because He knew that I would have much for which to say, "I am sorry," especially as a child. I would awake each morning, begging Him to help me to be good. I would arrive at breakfast, and right away I would slip. It seemed that I could never be as good as I really wanted to be. But, as I said, I was a good repenter. I am grateful for this because confession is also an important part of our prayer life. What freedom, to know that we can always go to Him, confess and repent of our sins and shortcomings, and know that He instantly hears and answers.

Through the years, I have also learned the joy

Photograph opposite: Sunset over the mountains of Montreat, N.C.

and privilege of praying for others. What a blessing it is to keep a little notebook with a prayer list. I have a small black notebook and on each page, the day of the week is written on the top. Under each day, I have listed the persons for whom I wish to pray. For example, one day might be devoted to those women friends of mine who are single parents, another to friends who have not as yet experienced this personal relationship with Christ, one day devoted to family, etc. I write the name in one column, the request in the next column, and then the answer and the date of the answer in the third column. What a blessing and encouragement to look back at the answers to prayer.

The most exciting answer to prayer that I see is to look back over the years and see how God has worked in my own life, to see the changes, no matter how small. I can see how He has faithfully directed and guided me, how He has blessed and used each circumstance for His glory. I am still a student in the school of prayer and there is much that I have yet to learn; but what I have already experienced makes me eager for more. Prayer is a source of real power. Someone once said, "Men may spurn our appeal, reject our message, oppose our arguments, despise our persons, but they are helpless against our prayers."

Come, My Soul

Come, my soul, thy suit prepare,
Jesus loves to answer prayer;
He Himself has bid thee pray,
Therefore will not say thee nay.

Thou art coming to a King,
Large petitions with thee bring;
For His grace and power are such,
None can ever ask too much.

John Newton

Not in Vain

Not in vain the tedious toil
On an unresponsive soil,
Travail, tears in secret shed
Over hopes that lay dead.
All in vain, thy faint heart cries,
Not in vain, thy Lord replies;
Nothing is too good to be;
Then believe, believe to see.

Did thy labor return to dust?
Suffering did it eat like rust?
Till the blade that once was keen
As a blunted tool is seen?
Dust and rust my life's reward?
Slay the thought: Believe thy Lord,
When thy soul is in distress
Think upon His faithfulness.

Amy Carmichael

Photograph opposite: The author holding her sixth child.

His Plan for Me

When I stand at the judgment seat of Christ
And He shows me His plan for me,
The plan of my life as it might have been,
Had He had His way; and I see

How I blocked Him here, and I checked Him there,
And I would not yield my will,
Will there be grief in my Savior's eyes,
Grief, though He loves me still?

He would have me rich, and I stand there poor,
Stripped of all but His grace,
While memory runs like a hunted thing
Down the paths I cannot retrace.

Then my desolate heart will well nigh break
With tears that I cannot shed;
I shall cover my face with my empty hands;
I shall bow my uncrowned head.

Lord of the years that are left to me,
I give them to Thy hand;
Take me and break me, mold me to
The pattern Thou hast planned.

Martha Snell Nicholson

In the Cross of Christ I Glory

In the cross of Christ I glory,
Towering o'er the wrecks of time;
All the light of sacred story
Gathers round its head sublime.

When the woes of life o'er take me,
Hopes deceive, and fears annoy,
Never shall the cross forsake me:
Lo! It glows with peace and joy.

When the sun of bliss is beaming
Light and love upon my way,
From the cross the radiance streaming
Adds more luster to the day.

Bane and blessing, pain and pleasure,
By the cross are sanctified;
Peace is there that knows no measure,
Joys that through all time abide.

In the cross of Christ I glory,
Towering o'er the wrecks of time;
All the light of sacred story
Gathers round its head sublime.

John Bowring

Photograph above: The author with her husband and their six children.

Obedience

Abiding through time spent in the Living Word and through time spent in prayer, in fellowship with the person of Jesus Christ, has been vital in my Christian walk and in my spiritual growth. There is another aspect that has been just as important and just as vital, and that is obedience, simple obedience. In 1 Samuel we read that to "obey is better than sacrifice." The Scriptures are filled with verses dealing with the cursings of disobedience and the blessings of obedience. In Jeremiah 7:23-24, we read, "But this thing commanded I them, saying, Obey my voice, and I will be your God, and ye shall be my people: and walk in all the ways that I have commanded you, that it may be well unto you. But they hearkened not, nor inclined their ear, but walked in the counsels and in the imagination of their evil heart, and went backward, and not forward."

It seems very clear to me that if I am to go

forward, then I must obey, and it is by obedience that one learns to obey. There are many blessings in Scripture associated with, and a direct result of, obedience, among which are blessings of prosperity, long life, success, safety. But the reason that I wish to live in obedience is because it brings glory to God and is an evidence of my love for Him. First John 5:3 says, "For this is the love of God, that we keep His commandments: and His commandments are not burdensome." I am free and fulfilled because of Christ's obedience. He became "obedient unto death" for me, so how much more should I obey Him? For me obedience is a privilege. It is not always easy, but He gives the power and strength to follow any commandments or instructions that He has made. In the years that I have, by His grace, made it a practice to obey Him, I have found that it is always for my good. As I saturate myself in His Word, listen to Him, and spend time seeking His will and His plan, He speaks, He directs, and I seek to obey.

"How can men be wise? The only way to begin is by reverence for God. For growth in wisdom comes from obeying His laws."

Proverbs 24:3-4 says, "Through wisdom is a house builded, and by understanding it is established; And by knowledge shall the chambers be filled with all precious and pleasant riches." I have found that the kind of true wisdom that it takes to build a home can only come from God. "But the wisdom that

Photograph opposite: Contentment is in knowing "All is well between us."

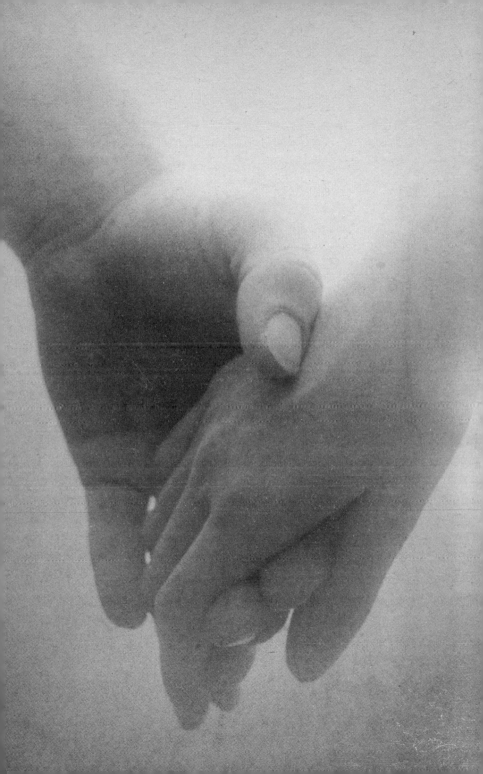

comes from heaven is first of all pure and full of quiet gentleness. Then it is peace-loving and courteous. It allows discussion and is willing to yield to others; it is full of mercy and good deeds. It is wholehearted and straightforward and sincere" (James 3:17, Living Bible). What a beautiful picture of a Christian home, but it takes a lot more than I or my husband have put together to achieve this kind of atmosphere. So far, our home fails in all but the "allows for discussion, and the wholehearted and sincere." None of us are full of quiet gentleness, and it is hard for the kids to see the value of "yielding" to each other. Perhaps neither I nor my husband have this kind of wisdom, but we can call on the One who does.

"Through understanding it is established." This is where I believe that communication is so vital. There is limited understanding where there is little communication, and communication takes lots of time. Someone said that "A child's life is now." How true this is. There are times when the voices and "communication" of six children, often at the same time, wear me out, and it is then that I have to remind myself of the vital importance of this open communication and the knowledge of my children that it cultivates. Taking the time to really know and understand my family and their needs fills the home with "rare and beautiful" treasures, with "all precious and pleasant riches": the love, the joy, the

Photograph opposite: The Graham family at home.

happiness, the understanding, the acceptance, the security, the direction.

All these precious and rare treasures, and more, I received in my little home in Montreat, North Carolina, and now I am, with the help of the Lord Jesus, passing these priceless treasures on to my children. Why have a home? For all these reasons and many more, I am so grateful to have a home. I chose to have my own home, and I have never regretted this decision. Simply put, I love it; but more than this, I find such a joy in being a vital part of the very first institution that God created.

A beautiful gift edition of THANK YOU, LORD, FOR MY HOME is available by Ideals Publishing. This full-color, 8½ x 11 paper cover edition is available in bookstores everywhere or by mail from Grason Company, Box 1240, Minneapolis, MN 55440. Please request the IDEALS edition and enclose $5.95 in check or money order.